# Bright Hea

## Inspirational Stories About Bravery, Positivity, and Kindness

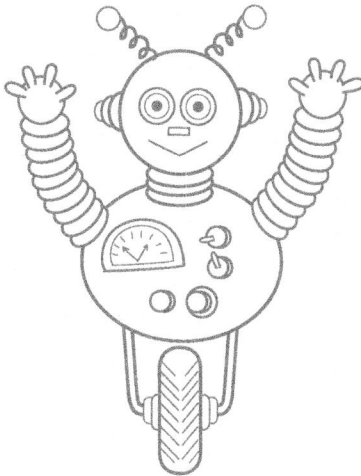

Brightheartbooks.com

# Table of Contents

Introduction ...**v**

New Hellos ...**1**

Eleventh Time's the Charm ...**13**

The Prince and the Village Boy ...**27**

Henry's First Cat ...**41**

John Puts On a Show ...**53**

Brian Conquers His Book Report ...**65**

Victor Struggles With His Grades ...**77**

Conclusion ...**86**

About Bright Heart ...**89**

# ~~$10~~ FREE BONUS
# COLORING BOOK FOR KIDS

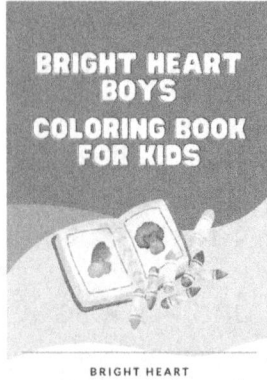

BRIGHT HEART

## Unleash your creativity with our printable coloring book.

Inside the Coloring Book for Kids, you will find:

- The seven "I" message illustrations from the heartwarming "Bright Heart Boys" book, ready to be brought to life with your own vibrant colors.
- Beautifully crafted illustrations straight from the pages of the "Bright Heart Boys" book, capturing the magic and wonder of the tales.
- The convenience of a printable format – ideal for both at-home and classroom use.

Scan the QR code below to claim your copy.

OR

Visit the link below:

## http://brightheartbooks.com/brightheart-bonus

# Introduction

Dear Parents,

Do you want to inspire your boys to become their best selves? Are you looking for a way to teach your boys important values like perseverance, gratitude, goal-setting, and self-care?

Well, this book is just what you need! Inside these pages, you'll find a collection of inspiring stories about boys who faced their fears, tried their best, and never gave up. These stories will teach your boys important values that they can apply to their own lives, and they'll show them that anything is possible when they believe in themselves.

At the end of each story, your boys will find a special "I" message that encourages them to apply what they've learned to their own lives, as well as a beautiful coloring illustration that lets them express their creativity and imagination. And throughout the book, they'll be reminded that they are loved, accepted, and valued just the way they are, even in the most difficult

moments of their lives.

To make it even better, you can easily download and print the illustrations by scanning the QR code or visiting the link on page iv, so your boys can enjoy them again and again!

So if you want to inspire your boys to become the amazing boys they were born to be, get your hands on this book and start reading with them. Let these stories inspire, motivate, and empower them to be their best selves. And always remember: your boys are amazing, and the world needs them and their unique gifts!

Sincerely,

Bright Heart

Hey there, amazing boys!

I hope you're excited to read the stories in this book and learn how to be your best self. Remember, sometimes life can be hard and you might face challenges that seem really big. But don't worry, you have everything you need inside of you to overcome those challenges and achieve your dreams. You're unique and special, and that's what makes you amazing!

As you read each story, try to think about what you can learn from the boy in the story. Maybe you'll learn about trying your best, or being kind to others, or never giving up. And don't forget to look at the "I" message and coloring illustration at the end of each story. These are special messages just for you that will help you remember what you learned and let you express your creativity!

Get ready to be inspired by these amazing stories. You've got this, and I believe in you!

Sincerely,

Bright Heart

# New Hellos

Martin liked to be a happy boy, but sometimes it seemed impossible. Sometimes it seemed as if the whole world was against him. Like everything and everyone in his life just wanted to make him miserable. Some days, it felt impossible to smile. Today was one of those days.

Dad had come home from work with some terrible news. His boss at work had asked him to

move to a different city, and he had agreed. That meant that Martin's life was about to change in almost every way. The friends he had worked so hard to make would now live hundreds of miles away. The school that he had gotten so used to would now be forgotten. And the life that he had grown to love would be lost.

He sat in the living room with his arms crossed, refusing to look up at the TV, even though his favorite show was on. "It's just not fair!" he mumbled. "I didn't ask for this to happen."

He spoke quietly, but his father heard him. "Sometimes things are out of our control, Martin. Sometimes you just have to go with the flow in life." Martin frowned and did his best to look even madder. "And besides," his father continued, "a new city means new experiences. You'll go to a new school and make new friends. You'll learn new things and find new hobbies. It'll be perfect! You'll see."

Martin hated it when people tried to make terrible situations seem good. He frowned even harder and grunted.

Martin had one more week at school before the big move. He told his friends the terrible news, and they made him feel better by telling him how terrible it was. They played their last games of tag and capture the flag together, telling stories about good times they had shared with each other.

Martin's friends thought these stories would make him happier, but instead he just got sadder. He hated to think of all the good memories they had had, but even more, he hated to think of all the good memories they would have without him.

When he got home from school, he was in an even worse mood than the day before. It was Mom's turn to try to cheer him up. "Martin, honey," she began, "what use is moping around? We have to move, so we might as well smile while we do it."

Martin was poking at his dinner with his fork, wondering if the food in this new city would be the same. "Why would I smile? This is a terrible situation!"

Martin's mom chuckled to herself and patted him on the back. "This isn't a terrible situation, Martin. This is life. In life, things change and we must change too. Sometimes stepping out of your comfort zone is the best thing you can do for yourself."

Martin grunted and squished a pea with his fork.

"You'll see," his Mom said and she left the room.

Martin said his goodbyes to his friends and his teachers and his school. The big move was that weekend.

Mom and Dad bustled around downstairs, packing boxes and moving furniture around.

Martin sat in his room, throwing clothes in the direction of his bag and sorting through old toys. His parents told him that he would have to get rid of half of his toys so they could fit everything in the moving truck—another terrible thing about the big move.

Early the next morning, the big moving truck pulled away from the curb and Martin peered out the window at his home one last time. He tried not to cry, but when he thought of everything he was leaving, he couldn't help it.

The new city was only four hours away, but to Martin, it felt like the trip took days. He felt like his old life was on another planet.

When Mom, Dad, and Martin pulled up to their new house, Martin smiled for the first time in a week. He didn't know why, but something made him happy. The house looked a lot like his old house, and the yard looked the same as well, but something made him smile. This house was new to him. He had never seen it before and that was exciting.

His smile disappeared, however, when he remembered that he would have no one to play in his yard with. He had no friends.

When the truck was unloaded and the family sat down for their first dinner at their new house, Martin's smile was gone. Once again, he sat in silence and poked at the food on his plate. His parents had made his favorite meal to cheer him up. He didn't let it.

When the silence had gone on long enough, Martin's father spoke. "You know, Martin, there is a lot of power in changing your mindset.

Moving could be a terrible thing—it could mean leaving everything you love and everyone you know. Or it could be a wonderful thing—it could mean having great new experiences and meeting the best new friends."

Martin didn't look up, but deep down, he heard his father's words. He thought about them that first night in bed. He thought about his old friends and how much he missed them. He

thought about his favorite teacher and how far away she was now. But he also thought about the new friends he hadn't met yet and the new teachers he would have. He thought about the yard outside his house, but instead of picturing himself playing alone, he saw himself with a lot of wonderful friends.

When he woke up the next day, he felt very different than the past week. He ran downstairs to breakfast whistling his favorite song. "Hi, Mom! What's for breakfast?"

Martin's mother raised her eyebrows and embraced her son. "We don't have much, so you'll have to eat cereal!"

Martin smiled and skipped to the cupboard to grab a bowl. "Fine with me." He peeked through the curtains at the morning sun and smiled. It was a new day.

Dad was out running errands for most of the day and was surprised when he returned home to find Martin playing soccer in the yard with a neighbor boy. He waved to his son and Martin ran over to give him a hug. "Nice to see a smile

on your face. What've you been up to today?"

Martin pointed at the boy over his shoulder. "That's Mitch. He lives across the street and his favorite sports are soccer and basketball just like mine." Mitch ran over and introduced himself to Martin's father. Martin continued, "Mitch says that every Saturday his family has a barbecue and all of us are invited."

Martin was gone before his father could reply, whooping and sprinting across the yard.

When school started, Martin was excited. He

had a friend, Mitch, and that made everything a lot less scary. Mitch introduced Martin to his group of friends and before long, Martin began to wonder if this new school would be a nice change after all. He missed his old friends and his old life, but he was starting to see that he could find the same things in this new life.

When Saturday came, Martin was floating in Mitch's pool, looking around at his new life. His parents shook hands with Mitch's parents and smiled.

Maybe the fresh start was just what he needed. Maybe these new friends could make him feel just as happy as the friends he had grown up with back home. Martin realized that a new life just meant new chances. He could keep his old friends back home. He could visit them and even introduce them to his new friends. He hadn't lost anything.

There was so much opportunity in this new life, but Martin wouldn't have noticed it if he had decided to stay sad. Martin learned many new things in this new life of his, but most of all, one lesson stuck with him. He learned

that his problems didn't seem so terrible when he stopped thinking about them all the time. By choosing to think positively rather than negatively, he had made his life happier.

# I STAY POSITIVE IN ANY SITUATION

# Eleventh Time's the Charm

Every boy and girl knows exactly what they want to be when they grow up. Some want to be doctors to save lives and make people healthy. Others want to be construction workers and build huge buildings to light up the sky. Some even want to be astronauts and see what strange things lie in outer space.

Jonah knew exactly what he wanted to be

from when he was four years old. On his fourth birthday, his grandfather bought him a book. On the front was a little boy with curly brown hair (Johan's was curly and brown as well) and a huge smile on his face. His eyes were looking up at the bright blue sky and in his hand, he held a string. The string went from the boy's hand high into the sky where it was attached to a beautiful red kite.

Jonah had never seen a kite before and he was fascinated. He couldn't believe that something that looked so big could float in the sky on its

own. He knew that to believe that this "kite" could actually fly in the sky, he would have to see it.

And so, a week after his birthday, his grandpa took him to the store to buy a kite. They found a beautiful green kite, brought it home, and waited.

"Why can't we fly today?" Jonah asked his grandpa. They were sitting at the breakfast table staring out at the beautiful blue sky. Jonah didn't understand why such a beautiful day was not a good day for kite flying.

His grandpa pointed to the trees. "See how the trees sit still?" he said. "That's because there is no wind. A kite needs wind to fly."

And so they waited.

When a windy day finally came around, Jonah was the most excited boy. He jumped up and down at the breakfast table, staring at the trees bending and swaying back and forth.

When he and his grandpa finally got that kite into the sky, Jonah could not believe his eyes. It actually did fly! The book was telling the truth!

The wind carried the kite all on its own!

Jonah whooped for joy and tugged at the string, guiding the green kite high above.

It sailed, swooped, and spun, and ... crash!!!

The beautiful green kite smashed into a tree and was torn and broken to pieces. Jonah let go of the string and watched the poor thing stuck high in the treetops.

It made him sad. Grandpa offered to go buy a new kite from the store, but Jonah told him not to. He didn't want to see another kite ruined at the top of a tree. "I need a kite that won't get stuck in the top of a tree," he told his grandpa. "I need a kite that can sail higher than all the other kites."

"We can go to the kite shop," said Grandpa. "They have much bigger and better kites than the normal store where we got this green one."

"No," said Jonah. "I'll build my own. I'll make the most beautiful kite of all."

From that day on, Jonah knew that he wanted to be a kite maker.

He started saving all of his money and gathering

supplies. Soon enough, he had everything he needed to build his first kite. *This kite*, he thought to himself, *will be the king of all kites. It will sail higher, farther, and faster than any other kite.*

He spent days measuring out the frame, cutting fabric, and gluing. At last, after hours of effort, he had a red kite just like the one from the book. It was tall and wide and it looked proud sitting there on his desk in his room. He knew that this kite was special.

Then came the hard part: the wait.

Each day, he woke up early in the morning and looked out the kitchen window. He hoped to see the trees swaying back and forth in the wind, but they were always still.

After a week, his beautiful red kite still sat on his desk and the trees outside stood still. *How can I test my kite*, thought Jonah, *if I don't have any wind?*

Then, as if the wind heard his thoughts, a strong breeze blew the next day. Jonah gathered his kite carefully in his arms and rushed outside. He took the string in his hand, held the kite in the

air, and began to run. The string was long and strong and Jonah knew that this kite wouldn't hit the tree like the green kite.

He ran and ran and ran and ran, but the kite just dragged along behind him. After a minute, he stopped running and put his hands on his knees. He breathed hard and looked back at the beautiful red kite laying on the ground. Why wouldn't it fly?

After trying ten more times, Jonah realized that the kite was too heavy. The fabric he had used would never be able to fly. He kicked the ground in anger and walked back inside, stuffing the beautiful kite under his bed.

He almost gave up on his dreams of being a

kite-maker that day, but something told him not to quit. After all, making a kite was not an easy thing to do.

And so, after a few days, he began to make his second kite. *This one*, he thought, *will be the king of the skies.*

He made it out of paper instead of fabric because he had learned his lesson. He knew that fabric was too heavy to fly. He was thankful that his first kite taught him this lesson.

When the second kite was finally ready, Jonah was just as excited as that first day with his grandpa. The trees outside swayed in a strong wind and the sun shone high in the sky. Jonah ran outside with his new kite, held it in the air, and began to run.

The kite shot into the air immediately and began to swoop and dart around like a bird. Jonah jumped with joy and laughed out loud, staring up at his beautiful kite. Then, suddenly, the wind blew a strong blast and the kite shot toward the ground. Jonah tried to save it, but it smashed into the hard dirt with a crash. When he reached it, it

was broken and bent in every way.

He stared at the poor kite broken on the ground for a few minutes, then picked it up and walked inside. He put it under his bed with the kite made of fabric and sat at his desk, staring at the wall. *I guess kite-making just isn't for me*, he thought to himself. *I should have known that the wind was too strong!*

The next day, when his grandpa asked about the kite, Jonah told him that he was done making kites. He would find a new dream.

His grandpa smiled. "But you've only tried twice, Jonah! You know what they say: 'third time's the charm!'"

Jonah decided that he would listen to his grandfather and try just one more time.

And so, the next day he started on his third kite. This time, he knew just what to do and the kite was ready in two days. He knew to make it out of paper because the first kite had taught him that fabric is too heavy. He also knew that he needed to be patient with the wind and wait for the right time because the second kite had

taught him how dangerous a strong wind can be for a kite.

When the day came to fly the third kite, Jonah was very careful. But when the breeze finally caught the kite, the glue came undone and the wooden frame split off from the paper. The kite crashed down once again.

Jonah was very upset. He thought that the third time would surely be the last time, but it wasn't. He promised himself that he would do whatever it takes to make and fly the perfect kite.

He made the fourth kite the next day. When he tried to fly it, however, the string broke and the

kite sailed away into the sky.

He made a fifth kite but the wooden frame came apart just like the third because he didn't wait long enough for the glue to dry.

He made a sixth kite but it tore on the door handle as he was running outside with it.

He made a seventh kite but the wind was too weak and it came crashing down to the ground.

He made an eighth kite but his dog tore it to shreds, thinking it was a new toy.

He made a ninth kite but after only a few seconds in the air, a clumsy bird smashed into it and tore a hole in the paper.

He made a tenth kite but it came crashing down to the ground for some reason that Jonah did not know.

Then, refusing to give up, Jonah made an eleventh kite. He made it with paper and glued it well, letting the glue dry and harden because he knew that the wind would tear apart a kite that was not well built. He tucked the kite carefully under his bed and waited patiently for

the perfect wind because he knew that a wind that was too strong would tear the kite to pieces and a wind that was too weak could not lift it into the air.

When the perfect wind came, he carried his beautiful kite carefully outside, making sure not to catch it on the door handle. Then, he held it carefully in the air and began to run.

After a few moments, the gentle breeze lifted the kite into the air and it began to fly. He flew it high and far and fast. Higher and farther and faster than any kite before.

This kite was the king of the skies because Jonah had learned from each of his past attempts and failures. He knew that to succeed in anything, you must be able to fail and keep on trying.

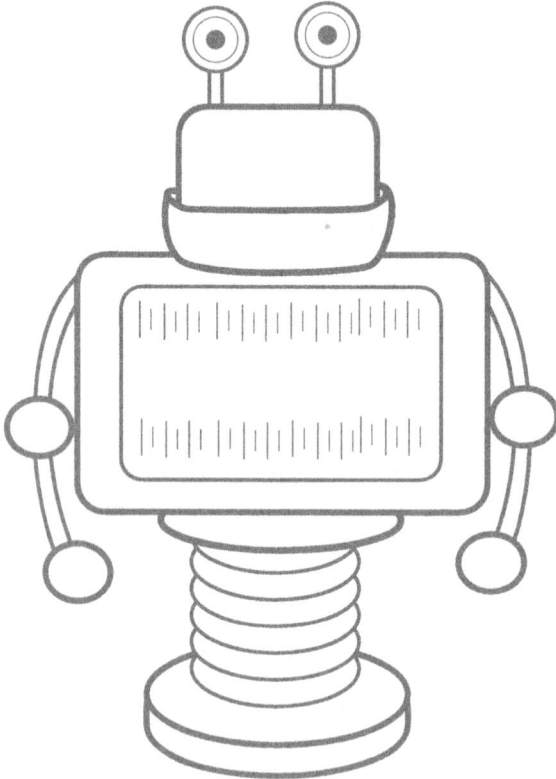

# I WILL KEEP TRYING

# The Prince and the Village Boy

There was once a kingdom in a land that no one remembers. In this kingdom stood a tower on a high hill. In this tower lived the king and queen, their servants, and their only son. The king and queen loved their son very much and gave him everything he wanted. No matter how much they gave him, however, it never seemed that he was happy.

The boy's name was Dartanion.

Dartanion had rooms full of toys, the best food in all the land, and ten servants waiting to give him anything he asked for. If he was bored, Dartanion would say, "Bring me my toy sword," and he would have it in his hand in a few seconds.

If he was hungry, he would say, "Make me a roasted duck," and the duck would be sitting in front of him in minutes.

He had friends that would visit him every day, a nanny to get him dressed, and any pet he wanted.

But Dartanion was not happy. What his parents didn't understand was that he didn't care about food or toys or friends. He loved having them all, of course, but what he really wanted was something else.

Above all things, Dartanion wanted freedom.

Each morning, when the sun had just risen and the sky was still dim, he would go to his bedroom window and look out over all the land. The tower he lived in was high, and he could see everything for miles around. He could see the river that wound its way through the valley and the town below. He could see the horses plowing the fields. On a clear day, he could even see the high mountains far away.

All he wanted was to explore these things he saw with his own two feet. He had read many stories about adventurous people, but these were just

stories to him. He wanted to swim in the river himself. He wanted to run on the dusty roads without worrying about getting his expensive clothes dirty. He wanted to laugh and play and wander as every other child did.

But, no. Dartanion was the prince and the prince couldn't do any of these things. When the prince played, he was watched by ten servants. When he ate, there was a cook at the door to make sure everything tasted good. There was no freedom in this life and Dartanion was tired of it.

In the town far below, lived another boy. This boy, like Dartanion in the tower high above, was not happy. His parents treated him well and he was never too hungry, too thirsty, or in any sort of danger. But he wanted things that he didn't have, and this made him unhappy.

His name was Michael.

Each morning, when the sun had just risen and the sky was still dim, Michael would crawl out of bed and walk over to his small window. He would pull apart the curtains and look out. While Dartanion would look down on the land

far below, Michael liked to look up. He would look up at the tower that stood high on the hill.

He would think of how wonderful it would be to live in this tower. He would imagine what it was like to have servants and to eat whatever he wanted to eat whenever he wanted to eat it. He had rice or porridge for most meals, but he knew that if he lived in that tower, he would have anything he wanted. He knew that he would wear fancy clothes and that his bed would be as soft as a baby kitten. Michael slept on a hard cot with one small blanket.

After he was done staring up at the beautiful tower and imagining another life, he would put on his old shoes, grab his little cap, and run outside to play with all the other kids. They would run over the hills and dusty roads without worrying about getting their clothes dirty. They would jump in the river and go fishing without any adults watching. It was always fun, but Michael wanted more. He wanted to have what the people who lived in the tower had.

One day, when Dartanion was out with his nurse on his morning walk, he spotted Michael.

Michael had his shoes on and his little cap and was running down the road, not worried about getting his clothes dirty. When Dartanion smiled at Michael, Michael stopped running.

"Aren't you the prince?" Michael asked Dartanion.

Dartanion nodded.

"That means," continued Michael, "that you live in that high tower!"

Dartanion nodded. He was confused why this village boy seemed so excited.

"What's it like to have everything you ever wanted in life?" asked Michael.

The nurse was impatient to move on from this talkative village boy, but Dartanion wanted to stay. He was the prince, so the nurse listened.

Dartanion looked at the strange boy and didn't answer his question. "Do you live in the town?" he asked.

Michael nodded.

Dartanion smiled. "That means you get to play wherever you want! You can run on dirt roads without worrying about your clothes getting dirty! You can swim in the rivers whenever you want! What's it like to be able to do whatever you want?"

Michael was very confused.

They walked and talked for a few minutes more and after begging the nurse, they came to an agreement. Because they both wanted each other's lives so much, they agreed to spend two days together.

On the first day, Dartanion would have the chance to follow Michael around and live life in the town as he did. And on the second day, Michael would go to the tower and live life as Dartanion did for a day.

The boys thought it was a good plan and were very excited for the next day.

Dartanion showed up at Michael's door with the biggest smile on his face. Michael's parents were amazed to see the young prince and bowed as they welcomed him in.

They started to prepare their best food, but Dartanion stopped them. "Is this what you normally eat?" he asked.

Michael's parents frowned. "No. Normally, we eat porridge or rice."

Dartanion smiled. "I want porridge or rice. I want to live Michael's life."

The boys ate porridge that morning, Michael laughing at Dartanion's face the whole meal. Dartanion had never had such bland-tasting food.

When they went out to play, Dartanion whooped with joy and ran over the dirt roads with the biggest smile on his face. They swam in the river and chased cows and did everything that Dartanion had dreamed of.

When they returned to Michael's home Dartanion asked, "What kind of toys do you have?"

"I don't really have any toys," Michael said. "I always just play outside. If I'm at home I usually help my family with chores."

"Oh," said Dartanion with a frown.

When lunch came around, Dartanion was disappointed to see that they were having rice. He didn't complain, however, because princes have good manners.

Dinner was porridge again and when they went to bed, Dartanion's stomach growled. He was used to having as much food as he wanted, but here, he only ate what he was given. I could really use a pineapple right now! he thought to himself. But he didn't complain.

When the boys went to bed, they laid down on their hard cots with one blanket. Dartanion couldn't sleep because he had never slept on something so hard before. His stomach growled, his feet felt dirty, and he thought about home in the high tower.

In the morning, Michael and Dartanion woke up and walked to the high tower on the hill that looked out over the town. They were let in and led to Dartanion's room.

Michael couldn't believe his eyes. He had never been somewhere so fancy. There were servants dressed in the nicest clothes at every doorway and Dartanion's bed was as big as his whole room.

When the servant came with their breakfast, Michael's jaw dropped. He had never seen so much delicious food. He ate it all with a smile on his face, thinking about how wonderful a life Dartanion lived. When he asked for a toy, it was in his hands in seconds and if wanted to pet a dog, the fluffiest dog was brought up to the room in minutes.

But soon, Michael got bored. "Can't we go outside and play?" he asked Dartanion.

"No," replied the prince. "The prince can't go outside with all the other children."

And so they sat in the high tower and played together with all the toys they could ever want.

When it came time to go to bed, another bed was brought into Dartanion's room. It was as soft as a kitten and Michael fell asleep in seconds.

When the sun rose in the morning, the boys woke up and looked out the high tower window together. They both wanted to go play in the town below, but they knew that's not what a prince should do.

"You know what?" began Michael. "Being in this high tower has been really fun. The food is good, there are as many toys as I want, and the bed is as soft as a kitten. But I do miss my home and playing whenever I wanted, wherever I wanted."

Dartanion nodded. "And I liked living in your home. We could do what we wanted and go where we wanted without being watched by

servants. But I did miss my good food and my soft bed and all of my toys."

"It's made me realize," said Michael, "that there are a lot of good things in my life that I never thought about before. I never thought about how fun it is to run in the fields and to go wherever I want. I am grateful for my freedom, even if my life is not as comfortable as yours."

"And I," began Dartanion, "didn't realize what a nice life I have high in this tower. I wish I had your freedom, but I like the comforts I have that many people don't. From now on, I'll be more grateful."

The boys stared out over the town for another hour, telling stories about their lives growing up. They were both grateful for everything they had.

# I'M GRATEFUL FOR WHAT I HAVE

# Henry's First Cat

Henry's big brother Max loved their new pet cat. He had named her Lucky. Lucky was black on her back and white on her belly. She liked to wander around the house, meow, and scratch at doors. Sometimes, she would lie on her back in the sun. When Max was around, she would crawl into his lap and purr.

Henry and Max had only gotten her a few days ago, and Max played with her nearly every day. Henry stayed far away from her, though. He was scared of the cat's sharp claws. What if it scratched him? When the cat ate, Henry could see that it had sharp teeth too. What if it bit him?

To avoid anything bad happening, Henry stayed in his room and lay next to his stuffed tiger. He took out his video game and played it while relaxing on his stomach, with his legs hanging off the foot of the bed. Sometimes, his big brother came and tried to play with him, but Henry always turned him away. He preferred playing by himself. One day, Max brought the cat with him, and as soon as he opened the door, Lucky ran into the room.

Henry was frightened. He jumped to the far side of the bed, pulling his legs up to his chest. Luckily, the cat did not jump onto the bed, but she looked up at Henry with curious eyes, and Henry's heart began to race. His palms suddenly felt sweaty. "Get it out!" he yelled.

Max approached Henry and the cat. "She just wants to say hi," he said.

Henry was panicky. He couldn't speak or think straight. His body was all tense and he started to shake. Max gave him an annoyed look. He picked up the cat, muttered something that went in one ear then out the other, and left. Once the door shut, Henry could finally breathe again. But a few minutes later, his mother came into the room.

Henry's mother was compassionate and gentle. She sat on the end of Henry's bed. Max had told her about what happened with the cat. She tried to reassure Henry, but Henry struggled to calm down. He just wanted the cat to leave him alone. He wished his brother had never brought the cat into his room. "Maybe it would be good for you to try and overcome your fear," Henry's mom suggested.

Henry shook his head. He couldn't imagine ever doing that. "No," he said. He felt panicky just thinking about it.

His mom nodded, saying she understood. "But cats aren't all scary," she said. "Sometimes, it's good to look on the positive side of things."

Henry didn't understand what his mom meant. The cat was too much. It was all scary. He told his mom that.

"What's scary?" his mom asked.

"What if the cat bites me?" Henry said. "Or scratches me? What if I get rabies? What if I

lose an eye?"

Henry's mother calmly answered every question. She explained how their cat had already been vaccinated for rabies, and how it had never scratched or bitten anyone before. It was safe. She told Henry that there was nothing to fear. "Just be gentle around her," Henry's mother said.

Henry still did not feel ready. But his mother reassured him that whenever he was ready, the cat would be ready too. "Just think of all the fun you could have with the cat," she said. "I bet she would love to purr in your lap. Her fur is very soft. And it's warm. It's different than touching your stuffed tiger."

When Henry's mother left, Henry began to think about the cat in a new way. He looked down at his stuffed tiger and thought about how the tiger was a type of cat too. Wouldn't it be nice to have a real cat in his lap? Henry wondered what it would feel like to have one purring beside him.

Henry still felt scared, though. He was so scared that even though he wanted to pet the cat, he

stayed away from it for the next few days. But even though he was avoiding the cat, he could not get it out of his mind.

Finally, one Saturday Henry decided it was time to come down from his room. When he got downstairs, he saw that his brother was petting the cat and his mom was on her iPad.

Henry went over to his mom and told her that he was ready to try petting the cat. His mother was supportive. "I am here for you," she said. "Come on, I will show you how to do it."

When Henry and his mother went over to the cat, his brother moved aside. "She's been waiting for you," he said.

Henry smiled and felt happy that everyone was supporting him. His mother demonstrated how to slowly approach the cat, letting it sniff her hand first. Then, she petted it. The cat wandered back and forth as she petted it, walking circles around her hand.

After a while, Henry saw how much fun his mom and the cat were having, and he decided he was ready to try it. However, when it came time

for Henry to pet the cat, he froze up. "I don't know if I can do it," he said.

His mother reassured him. "It's okay. The cat won't hurt you."

Henry mustered up all the courage he could find. He stuck out his hand. He was tense and nervous. He let the cat approach slowly. He petted it cautiously. His mom had been right. The cat was warm, and its fur was soft. It didn't try to scratch him or bite him. Henry relaxed just a little bit. After a moment, he petted the cat again. And again. And again after that.

The cat came closer to him, and that startled him. Henry jumped away from it, looking at it with fear in his eyes. The cat stared back at him with curiosity.

And then, it walked away.

It climbed up onto the sofa and lay down on it. It looked out the window, completely ignoring Henry!

Henry felt a pang of sadness now. "It doesn't like me," he said with worry.

His mother gently rubbed his back. "No, it likes you," she said. "Cats are just finicky."

His brother stood up. "Lucky, come on. Henry wants to play with you," he said.

Much to Henry's surprise, he picked up the cat by the torso. Its legs hung in the air as he carried it over and sat it down next to Henry.

Henry reached out and petted the cat. The cat

began to walk back and forth, letting him pet it. It felt so warm and soft. He kept petting it, and with time he began to relax and feel more comfortable. The cat was cute. Suddenly, Henry realized that he loved it.

His mother looked at him with a supportive expression on her face. "You see," she said, "the cat doesn't want to hurt you."

Henry's mother was right. Before, he'd only been able to see the cat for what it might do to hurt him. Now, he looked at it and saw how much it loved him.

Later, Henry went back to his room, and this time he brought Lucky with him. The cat climbed on his bed and lay by him. He sprawled out on his belly like before. This time, as he played his video game, the cat lay on one side of him, and his stuffed tiger on the other. Henry petted the cat and shared the warmth of his blankets with it. The cat snuggled next to him, and after a little while, it started to purr.

Henry had made a new friend. He felt glad that he'd given his new cat a chance.

I WILL BE BRAVE AND FACE MY FEARS

# Chapter "Good Will"

Helping others without expectation of anything in return has been proven to lead to increased happiness and satisfaction in life.

We would love to give you the chance to experience that same feeling during your reading experience today...

All it takes is a few moments of your time to answer one simple question:

**<u>Would you make a difference in the life of someone you've never met—without spending any money or seeking recognition for your good will?</u>**

If so, we have a small request for you.

If you've found value in your reading experience today, we humbly ask that you take a brief moment right now to leave an honest review of this book. It won't cost you anything but 30 seconds of your time—just a few seconds to share your thoughts with others.

Your voice can go a long way in helping someone else find the same inspiration and knowledge that you have.

Scan the QR code below:

OR

Visit the link below:

## https://geni.us/F1ZbBp

Thank you in advance!

# John Puts On a Show

John came from a family of actors. His mom and dad were always running around town, trying to get to rehearsals or performances for all the local theaters. John loved his parents. He thought they were really cool. He often went to see them perform with his grandmother, and he was in awe. His mom and dad dressed in fancy clothes on stage. They changed their voices and took on new names, and they performed, danced, and even sang with passion. Everyone

in the theater watched them, laughing, smiling, and having a good time. John loved clapping at the end of their performances. He wanted to be just like them.

One day, John was sitting in class next to his best friend Sam when their teacher told them they were going to put on a class play. John felt excited, because he realized that this was his chance to follow in his parents' footsteps. He couldn't wait to act on stage just like they did, and he couldn't wait for them to see him.

When John got home, he told his parents all about the upcoming class play. But as they began to ask questions, he started to feel nervous. Would he get a good part? Would he be able to memorize his lines? Would people like him? He was scared that he wouldn't be good enough and that he would let his parents down.

John told his parents what he was feeling, and they were very supportive. "No matter what, we're proud of you," his father said.

His mother reassured him as well. "I'm sure everyone will enjoy the performance," she said. "But if you want to do well, just make sure to work extra hard. Show your teacher how committed you are and give it your all!"

John took his parents' words to heart. The next day at school, he went up to her before class. He told her that he was excited to put on a good show and that he would give it his all, just like his mom had said!

His teacher smiled. She told John that she was glad to see that he was enthusiastic. "On Friday, you will get to audition," she said.

When Friday came, John and all his classmates were put in groups of four. His teacher gave them notecards with different roles and props. Every ten minutes, they swapped cards. John played a pirate first, then a king, then an old lady, and finally a merchant who sold apples. He worked hard to show off his acting, practicing different voices like he'd seen his parents do.

At the end of the day, his teacher said they would get their parts on Monday. John couldn't wait to start learning his lines. He was so giddy that he couldn't sit still on the bus home from school. And back at home, he was so excited that he started acting for his parents.

At dinner, he played a pirate, calling them "landlubbers" and responding with "aye, matey!" when they told him to put his dish in the sink.

On Saturday morning, he was an old lady with a bad back, walking down the stairs slowly, trying to find her medications before breakfast. Then, by the afternoon, he became a king. He sat in his father's green armchair, pretending it was a throne, and he wore a baseball cap as

his crown.

Then, on Sunday, he became a merchant. He took cookies, crackers, and peanuts out of the pantry and milk out of the fridge. He placed the food on the dinner table, then shouted to his parents in the other room. "Milk and cookies for sale! Crackers too! Come and get 'em! You won't find these prices anywhere else!"

His mother told him that she was glad to see he was working hard. "What you are doing is almost like method acting," she said.

John did not know what that was, so he asked about it.

His mother was happy to explain. "Method acting is when you prepare for a role by becoming the character in your day to day life."

John decided that he wanted to be a method actor.

The next day at school, his teacher handed out scripts for the school play and gave everyone their roles. John was excited and felt sure he would get a great role. When it came time for him to collect his script and see his part, the

teacher told him that he would be the king. He'd landed one of the leading roles!

John was thrilled with the role. But when he looked at the script, he realized that he had a lot of lines. John flipped through the script, counting them, and he began to feel overwhelmed. How would he ever memorize them all?

He went home to his parents and he showed them the script. He was feeling nervous. Would

he ever be able to perform like they did up on stage? Would he be able to live up to their expectations?

When they saw that he was cast as the king, they congratulated him. "We know you can do it," his mother said.

His father agreed. "Just make sure to work hard, and I'm sure you'll give everyone a good show!"

John really did want to give everyone a good show.

His mother nodded. "We'll help you learn your lines," she said. "So don't worry."

John was happy to see that his parents were proud of him. He put in a lot of hard work, just like his mom and dad had told him. He read over his script every night before bed, and he practiced the lines with his mom in the living room, speaking with a loud voice just like he would need to do on stage.

His mom and dad encouraged him, telling him that he was doing a good job preparing, just like a real stage actor. The encouragement gave John extra motivation, and he found it easier

to keep practicing, even when he got tired of reading lines.

Soon, it was time for the class play, and all of the parents came to watch. They sat in the back of the classroom, and John and other kids stepped outside with the teacher to prepare. John's friends Sam and Roy were playing his knights. As the king, John got to wear a big gold crown and a magnificent red cape. John, Sam, and Roy patiently waited for their turn while the

other kids performed inside the classroom.

John's friend Sam was nervous, so John tried to comfort him. "Don't worry. You only have one line, and if you forget it, I'll help you out, okay?"

Sam thanked John, but he didn't look any less nervous. When it was time for their first scene, John walked in confidently. In his first scene, he conversed with a band of pirates. When one of the pirates tried to attack, Roy stepped forward, protecting him. John put a hand on Roy's shoulder, just like the script said, and urged him to stay calm.

Later, John, Roy, and Sam appeared in a second scene, and John was able to deliver all of his lines in that scene too. As the play went on, he grew more comfortable saying his lines. John got into a rhythm. When it was time for Sam's line, John tried to make it easy for his friend: "Be on alert, Sir Sam," he said, adding the last part even though it wasn't in the script.

Sam delivered his line perfectly. "I shall protect your majesty with my life."

John was happy to see that his friend had done so well. When the play was over, his parents told him how proud they were. His teacher told the whole class that each and every one of them had exceeded her expectations. Then she asked everyone to give a special round of applause to John for his great performance as the king.

John was excited. His hard work had paid off. He'd been nervous that he might not be able to memorize all of his lines and that he might not live up to everyone's expectations, but he knew now that as long as he was willing to work hard, he could achieve anything.

# I CAN ALWAYS IMPROVE MYSELF BY PRACTICING

# Brian Conquers His Book Report

Brian loved reading, but he didn't love book reports. Everyone in his class had to write one, and he had no idea what to write. He usually got easy homework assignments, but this one was hard, because it had to be three whole pages! Brian had never worked on something this hard before, and he had no idea where to start. He felt lost, overwhelmed, and frustrated. He would have much preferred to draw some

pictures. He loved drawing the characters from his comic books and he was getting good at it. For three days straight, he drew comics instead of doing his book report. It was much easier.

But one day, while Brian was drawing his comics, he started to feel bad for avoiding his homework. The book report was due in two days, and he hadn't started it yet. Brian didn't want to disappoint his teacher, and he definitely didn't want to disappoint his parents. After he finished coloring the drawing of his superhero, Lord Brian, he got up from his desk and went to see his dad.

Brian's dad was in the kitchen, grabbing a snack from the fridge. He had just gotten home from work and was still in his dress clothes. He pulled out a leftover sandwich. "Hi, Brian," he said. "How are the comics coming along?"

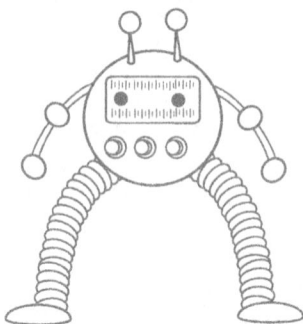

Brian's father knew he loved to draw. Brian could talk to him about comics for hours, but right now he needed help with his book report. He told his dad that the comics were coming along fine, but that he needed help with the homework assignment. He'd never had to work on such a hard assignment. "I can't write it," he told his dad. "It's too hard! It's supposed to be three pages, and I can't write that much."

Brian's father empathized with him. "I understand. Sometimes I feel the same way about my work. I have to solve hard problems every day."

Brian felt happy that his father understood him, but he was still lost and worried. What was he going to do about the book report?

His father continued. "When is your homework due?"

Brian answered truthfully. "In two days."

His dad responded with positivity. "That's plenty of time. Come with me, I'm going to help you."

Brian thought that maybe his dad would write the book report for him, but instead his dad sat Brian down at the computer. "When you set your mind to something, Brian, you can achieve anything," he said. He turned the computer on. "If it seems overwhelming, you just need to break it up into small goals. So, why don't we write one sentence for your book report?"

Brian didn't think one sentence would help. He told his dad that, but his dad insisted, so Brian wrote it.

Then, his dad told him to write a whole paragraph. Again, Brian argued. The report had to be three pages, not one paragraph! Brian was ready to give up, but his dad told him he was doing a great job. "Just trust me, and you'll get there," he said. "Imagine how good it will feel if this works. You'll have completed something really hard. Won't that be cool?"

Brian thought about it, and he agreed with his dad. He still didn't think that writing one paragraph would help, but he did it.

By the time he was done with the paragraph, he was finding it easier to write. His ideas were starting to flow. He wrote a third paragraph afterthat, and then a fourth paragraph. Soon, he had written a whole page.

His father beamed. "Wow, that was great work. I'm really proud of you, Brian."

Brian was amazed. He had written a whole

page of his book report. It was the hardest thing he'd ever had to do. He still had to write two more pages, but now he knew that he could do it.

His dad gave him a pat on the back. "Now that I helped you with one page of the book report, do you think you can write the rest on your own?" he asked.

Brian wasn't so confident, but he wanted to make his dad proud.

His dad praised him. "You did a great job with the first page," he said. "Just remember, you can break hard goals up into smaller goals. And if you get stuck again, you can always come to me for help."

Brian decided to try writing the rest on his own. He wrote another two paragraphs that night, and then he was tired so he went to sleep. The next day after school, he sat down and thought about drawing comics, but instead he worked on his book report.

At first, he had trouble thinking of things to write, but just like his dad had taught him, he focused

on one sentence first, and then one paragraph. Soon, it became easier for Brian to write. His fingers moved quickly over the keyboard. He relaxed. He reached the end of the second page, and there was just one more to go now.

Brian couldn't wait to finish the third page. He wanted to show his dad what he had accomplished. He was so proud of his new ability to work through hard things.

Brian wrote another paragraph. And then another. He was bouncing up and down in his chair now. It was almost done! A smile spread across his face as he wrote one more sentence.

And then, Brian reached the end of a very long paragraph, and he realized that he did not know what to write next. He tried really hard, but he couldn't think of a single good sentence.

Brian felt frustrated and upset. He did not know what to do, so he grabbed his colored pencils and started drawing. After a little while, he was so focused on the drawing that he forgot all about the book report!

The hours ticked by, and soon it was time for

dinner. He went downstairs and he ate with his mom and dad. When dinner was over, Brian decided to ask his dad for help. His dad was very supportive when Brian brought up the book report. "How can I help?" he wondered.

Brian told his dad that he was stuck. He'd only written a little more than two pages, and he couldn't think of anything else to say.

His dad made him feel better. "It's okay to get stuck," he said. "Why don't you try writing it like you're talking to me?"

Brian didn't understand what his father meant. His father explained more. "When you're passionate about something, Brian, you can talk for hours about it. Just try and pretend like you're talking out loud, and write what you would say in the book report."

Brian understood now. He told his dad that he would try it.

Brian sat down again and did as his father had said. When he thought about what he would say out loud, he realized that there was a lot of stuff he hadn't written yet. Brian's fingers glided

over the keyboard, and writing started to come easier for him.

He wrote one sentence. Then he wrote a paragraph. Then he wrote another paragraph.

Soon, Brian had written three whole pages! He felt excited. He smiled wide.

Just at that moment, his father came by with some cookies. "How is the book report going?" he asked.

Brian took two cookies and munched on them as he answered. "I finished it!" he said. He was so happy.

His father smiled and told Brian how proud he was. "You see, Brian. You can accomplish anything you want."

Brian smiled back at his father. He understood exactly what his father meant now. Even if a problem seemed really hard, he could always break it up into smaller goals in order to achieve it easier. And if that didn't work, he knew that his dad would always be there to help him out.

Brian wolfed down the last of the cookies. "Do you want to draw comics with me?" he asked his dad.

His father nodded. "Absolutely."

And with that, Brian got out his colored pencils, and he shared them with his father. This time, as he drew, Brian felt like a big success. He'd written his first book report. He could do anything he set his mind to.

# I AM CAPABLE OF ACHIEVING MY GOALS

# Victor Struggles With His Grades

Victor sat in front of his backpack, and he didn't want to open it. Earlier in the day, he had gotten his math test back from his teacher. He was supposed to show it to his parents, but he hadn't gotten a good grade. He knew that his mom and dad wouldn't be angry, but he was afraid of letting them down. His dad was very smart. Victor wanted to be as smart as him. His brother Oscar was smart too, and Victor felt like he needed to keep up.

After a tense moment, Victor opened his backpack and he took out the test. There was a big red C at the top of the test paper, along with a bunch of corrections in red. His brother always got A's. Victor felt bad about himself because he hadn't done better. He was stressed out. He was even angry at the teacher for not giving him a better grade. All the other kids had done better, including his best friend John. Victor felt like he must be stupid to get a C.

Victor knew he couldn't hide his grade from his parents, so he went to them with the test. He found his dad and mom in the kitchen and told

them he wanted to talk. They all sat down at the dinner table and Victor showed them the test.

His father could see how upset Victor was, and he spoke in a soft voice. "You did just fine," he said. "Did you study for the test?"

"Yes!" Victor said.

His mother put her arm around him, rubbing him gently. "All that counts is that you did your best."

Victor had done his best, and that was what made him so upset. He felt like his best wasn't good enough. "I feel stupid," he told his parents. "I feel like I'll never be as good as Oscar."

His mom looked at him with a loving expression on her face. "You and Oscar are both special in your own ways."

His dad nodded. "You're not stupid, Victor," he said. "Everyone struggles sometimes, and everyone struggles with different things. At work I face things that are hard for me all the time. When that happens, I just keep working hard, and do the best that I can. That's all we expect from you. We know you are trying hard and we're proud of you."

Victor's mother agreed with his father. "And if you're ever having trouble, you can always come to us for help. We'll always be here, Victor."

"I did try very hard," Victor said. He was beginning to see things in a different way.

Victor felt a little better knowing that his parents still thought highly of him, and that they were there for him. He went back to his room, because he had some additional math homework to do.

But after a while, he started to have trouble concentrating. He rocked back and forth in his chair, feeling like he wanted to be doing something else. Every thought in his brain felt jumbled, and he constantly read the problems over and over, struggling to remember what he'd just read.

Victor knew that something was wrong, but he didn't know what. He only knew that he couldn't concentrate. At first he felt angry. He tried to push himself harder, but that didn't work. Eventually, he got up, frustrated, and went downstairs to ask his parents for help.

Victor's dad was playing Scrabble on his iPad when Victor came to him. He set the game aside and listened intently as Victor told him that he was having trouble studying.

He nodded after Victor had finished explaining. "That happens to me sometimes, too," he said. "It means you've been working very hard. When you are having trouble concentrating like that, you need to take a break."

Victor was surprised. "Really?" he said, feeling

worried. "But I haven't finished studying yet."

Victor didn't want to take a break. He wanted to prove he could do better in math. However, his dad assured him that by taking a break, he would be able to recharge and he would have more energy later.

"It's important to work hard," his dad said. "But it's equally important to spend time having fun and relaxing, and you might just find that you learn more after you've had a chance to recharge. Come on, how about you and I take a walk to the store? Your mom needs a few things for dinner."

Victor and his dad walked to the local supermarket, stopping to talk with neighbors who were walking their dogs or just out enjoying the evening.

Dinner was ready shortly after they returned home. After dinner, Victor watched TV with his parents for a while and then went to bed. He didn't try to study any more that night. But the next day, Victor went back to studying what he had gotten wrong on the test again, and this time it was much easier to concentrate.

Victor started to feel good about himself again. He knew that he was trying his best, and that was what mattered. And he was confident that he would do better on the next test.

And sure enough, when it came time to take another math test, Victor was well prepared. He

had studied hard but also taken breaks when he needed to. He understood most of the material, and when he didn't, he asked his mom or dad for help.

When the teacher gave him back his graded test paper, he saw that he had gotten a B this time instead of a C.

Victor felt happy that he had improved, even though it was not the A he was hoping for. He had learned to be less hard on himself. And he understood that as long as he did his best, his parents would be proud of him.

# I WILL ALWAYS BELIEVE IN MYSELF

# Conclusion

For the parents,

Congratulations on finishing this book filled with inspiring stories and valuable life lessons! I hope these stories have helped your child realize that they are capable of achieving great things and that they have the strength and courage to overcome any challenge that comes their way.

Life can be full of ups and downs, but it's important to remember that your child is unique, loved, and important to this world. Encourage them to believe in themselves and trust that they can make a difference. Remind them to dream big, try their best, and take care of themselves by doing things that make them happy and strong.

The lessons learned from these stories, such as kindness, perseverance, and gratitude, can be applied to your child's everyday life. Encourage them to treat others with kindness, never give up on their dreams, and be thankful for the good things in their lives.

I'm proud of your child for taking the time to

read this book and for being open to learning new things. Keep encouraging them to read, learn, and grow into the amazing person they are meant to be. The world is waiting for them, and I know they will do great things!

Thank you for supporting your child on their journey to becoming their best selves.

Sincerely,

Bright Heart

For the amazing Boys,

You made it to the end of the book! Congratulations! I hope you enjoyed reading these inspiring stories and learned a lot from them. Remember, you are capable of great things and have the power to achieve anything you set your mind to.

Life can be tough sometimes, but don't forget that you are strong and brave. You can face any challenge that comes your way! Always remember to be kind to others, never give up on your dreams, and take care of yourself by doing the things that make you happy and healthy.

I hope you had fun coloring the illustrations too! Remember, you can always go back and color them again whenever you want. And don't forget to keep reading, keep learning, and keep growing into the amazing person you are meant to be! You are loved, you are special, and you can make a difference in this world. So go out there and show the world how amazing you are!

Sincerely,

Bright Heart

# About Bright Heart

Brightheartbooks.com is a website dedicated to inspiring and empowering children to become their best selves. It is made up of passionate writers, editors, and illustrators who share a deep commitment to creating books that help children develop key skills, such as creativity, empathy, and critical thinking.

Bright Heart values are at the heart of everything it does. It believes in the power of storytelling to connect people, inspire imagination, and promote positive change. It strives to create books that are inclusive, diverse, and reflective of the world around us. Above all, it believes in empowering children to see themselves as agents of change who are capable of making a difference in their own lives and communities.

Bright Heart books are designed to be both entertaining and educational, with engaging stories and chapters, playful illustrations, and valuable lessons that help children navigate the world around them. It aims to create books that children will love to read and that parents will

love to share with their children.

Thank you for choosing Bright Heart for your child's reading journey. We're honored to be a part of your family's story, and we hope our books bring joy, inspiration, and growth to your child's life.

If you have any questions, please feel free to email us at contact@brightheartbooks.com.


Thank you,

Bright Heart

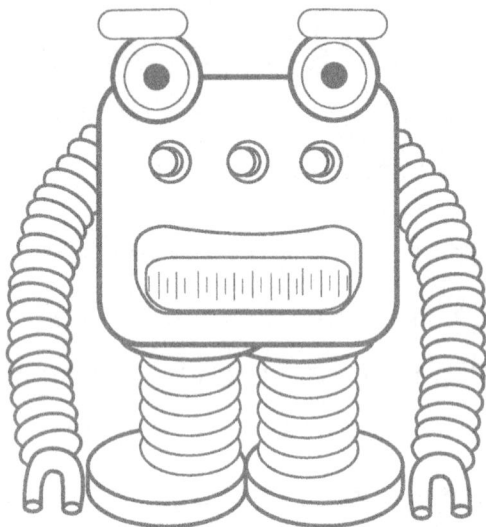

# Your opinion counts!

If you enjoyed this book, please consider leaving a review on Amazon and help other readers discover it.

Scan the QR code below:

OR

Visit the link below:

**https://geni.us/F1ZbBp**

Printed in Great Britain
by Amazon